I'M AN AMERICAN CITIZEN

Electing Our Leaders

Earl McGraw

PowerKiDS
press™

NEW YORK

Published in 2013 by The Rosen Publishing Group, Inc.
29 East 21st Street, New York, NY 10010

Book Design: Michael Harmon

Photo Credits: Cover, p. 18 Lisa F. Young/Shutterstock.com; cover (flag) Kanwarjit Singh Boparai/Shutterstock.com;
p. 4 Digital Vision./Thinkstock.com; p. 5 Photos.com/Thinkstock.com; pp. 6, 10, 15 iStockphoto/Thinkstock.com;
p. 7 Matthew Cavanaugh/Stringer/Getty Images News/Getty Images; p. 8 Karla Caspari/Shutterstock.com; p. 9 Diane
Macdonald/Photographer's Choice RF/Getty Images; p. 11 Paul Hudson/Getty Images; p. 12 Christopher Wilhelm/
Photographer's Choice/Getty Images; p. 13 Paula Bronstein/Stone/Getty Images; p. 14 Hill Street Studios/Blend Images/
Getty Images; p. 16 © iStockphoto.com/Miravision; p. 17 Digital Vision/Digital Vision./Getty Images; p. 19 Mike Flippo/
Shutterstock.com; p. 20 Paul Thompson/Stringer/Hulton Archive/Getty Images; p. 21 © iStockphoto.com/asiseeit.

Library of Congress Cataloging-in-Publication Data

McGraw, Earl.
 Electing our leaders / Earl McGraw.
     p. cm. — (I'm an American citizen)
 Includes index.
 ISBN: 978-1-4488-8842-9
 6-pack ISBN: 978-1-4488-8843-6
 ISBN: 978-1-4488-8583-1 (library binding)
1. Elections—United States—Juvenile literature. 2. Voting—United States—Juvenile literature. I. Title.
 JK1978.M39 2012
 324.60973—dc23
                            2012012059

Manufactured in the United States of America

CPSIA Compliance Information: Batch #WS12RC: For further information contact Rosen Publishing, New York, New York at 1-800-237-9932.

Word Count: 484

Contents

Why Do We Vote?

Do you know what it means to vote? When you vote for something, you pick it above everything else. You might vote in school. It tells your teacher what you want to do.

Voting is an important part of being an American. Americans vote to pick our leaders. We have to pick a lot of leaders for our country. Our leaders make rules and laws.

Our most important leader is the president. The president is the leader for the whole United States. This is a very important job.

We also have leaders in our towns and cities. We have leaders for our states, too. These kinds of leaders help **local** governments.

Elections

We vote for leaders during an **election**. We vote for our president every 4 years. This is the most important election in the United States. It happens in November.

We have elections to decide the leaders for towns
and cities. Sometimes we have elections at school.
These happen often.

Choosing Our Leaders

People who run in elections are called **candidates**.

Candidates spend a lot of time talking to people.

They tell us what they want to do for our country.

There can be many candidates in an election. It can be hard to pick the person you like the most. Do you know how we decide whom to vote for?

We decide how to vote by listening to what the
candidates say. They tell us how they feel about
our country. It's important to listen to every candidate.

Candidates make speeches to tell us their ideas.

A speech is a long talk in front of a lot of people.

We remember their ideas when it's time to vote.

We vote on Election Day. Sometimes we vote in a
voting **booth**. The voting booth keeps everyone's vote
a secret. This makes our elections fair.

Another way to vote is by filling out a form. We pick the candidate we like. Then we send the form in the mail. This way is a little slower, but it still works.

We find out who the winner is when everyone finishes voting. The person with the most votes wins!

The person who wins becomes our leader. Their job is hard, but it's very important. Sometimes we have the same leader for a long time.

Who Votes?

Voting is one way to be a good American. Every American has the chance to vote, but there are some rules. One rule is that you have to be 18 years old.

You also have to be a citizen. A citizen is someone who was born in the United States. Sometimes people from other countries can become citizens.

A long time ago, some Americans couldn't vote.

This was unfair. Many people wanted to change this.

They voted for leaders who helped change this rule.

Today, all Americans have the right to vote. Everybody can give his or her **opinion**. This is what makes our country great.

All About Voting!

who?	citizens
what?	picking a leader
where?	in a voting booth
when?	during an election
why?	to make our country a good place to live

Glossary

booth (BOOTH) A small closed space.

candidate (KAN-duh-dayt) Somebody who runs
   in an election.

election (ih-LEHK-shun) The act of picking a leader.

local (LOH-kuhl) Having to do with things that are
   near you.

opinion (uh-PIHN-yuhn) How you feel about something.

Index